Published in 2013 by The Rosen Publishing Group, Inc.
29 East 21st Street, New York, NY 10010

Copyright © 2013 Weldon Owen Pty Ltd. Originally published in 2011 by Discovery Communications, LLC

Photo Credits: **KEY** tl=top left; tc=top center; tr=top right; cl=center left; c=center; cr=center right; bl=bottom left; bc=bottom center; br=bottom right; bg=background

CBT = Corbis; DT = Dreamstime; GI = Getty Images; iS = istockphoto.com; SH = Shutterstock; TF = Topfoto; TPL = photolibrary.com; wiki = Wikipedia

front cover c DT; bg iS; **back cover** bc SH; tl TPL; **1**c TPL; **2–3**tc CBT; **4–5**c GI; **6**bc GI; **6–7**bg iS; **7**tc SH; br TF; **8**bc iS; bc, br SH; **9**tr, tr CBT; bc, tc iS; **10**bc, bl iS; **10–11**bc, bg iS; **11**bl iS; **12–13**bg iS; c TPL; **13**br TPL; **14–15**bg iS; **15**tr TPL; **16**br, cl, tr iS; c SH; bc, br TF; tl TPL; **17**bl, cr, tl iS; bc, br, tr SH; **18**cl iS; c, c, tr TF; **18–19**c CBT; bg iS; **19**tr CBT; cr TF; tl TPL; **20**bc iS; **20–21**c CBT; **22**cr iS; bc SH; br TPL; **22–23**bg iS; **23**tl TF; bl TPL; **24**bc DT; **24–25**bg iS; **25**tr CBT; tl iS; **26**c DT; bl, cl iS; bc SH; **26–27**bc DT; tc SH; **27**bc, cr, tc iS; cr wiki; **28**cl CBT; bl, cr TF; **29**br DT; tr TPL; **31**cr TPL; **32**bg iS

All illustrations copyright Weldon Owen Pty Ltd. **22**tr Andrew Davies/Creative Communications; **25**bc Lionel Portier

Weldon Owen Pty Ltd
Managing Director: Kay Scarlett
Creative Director: Sue Burk
Publisher: Helen Bateman
Senior Vice President, International Sales: Stuart Laurence
Vice President Sales North America: Ellen Towell
Administration Manager, International Sales: Kristine Ravn

Library of Congress Cataloging-in-Publication Data
Einspruch, Andrew.
 DNA detectives / by Andrew Einspruch. — 1st ed.
     p. cm. — (Discovery education: technology)
Includes index.
 ISBN 978-1-4488-7883-3 (library binding) — ISBN 978-1-4488-7965-6 (pbk.) —
ISBN 978-1-4488-7971-7 (6-pack)
1. DNA—Juvenile literature. I. Title.
QP624.E43 2013
572.8'6—dc23
                                        2011048221

Manufactured in the United States of America
CPSIA Compliance Information: Batch #SW12PK: For Further Information contact Rosen Publishing, New York, New York at 1-800-237-9932

Discovery
EDUCATION™

TECHNOLOGY

DNA DETECTIVES

ANDREW EINSPRUCH

PowerKiDS
press
New York

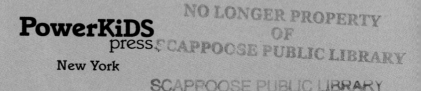

Contents

Passing on Traits

Every living thing on Earth—from plants to animals to bacteria—reproduces, or creates new versions of itself. In doing so, these living beings pass on traits, such as eye color or ear shape, from one generation to the next.

People have long understood that something like this goes on. They would look at a daughter and think, "She looks like her father." But it took decades of scientific discovery to figure out exactly how this passing on of inherited traits works. How does it happen that she has the same nose, eye shape, and height as her father? The answer is genes. These are the codes and instructions that transfer from parent to child, giving us what is called genetic inheritance.

That's Amazing!
When comparing human genes to chimpanzee genes, 96 percent are the same. This means that the differences come down to only 4 percent of our genes.

Traits across the generations
One of the interesting aspects of genes is that traits do not necessarily show up in each generation. A trait can be passed down from a grandparent to a parent to a child. It can be seen in the grandparent, and while it may not be expressed in the parent, it is visible again in the child.

Eyes
Eye color is inherited, but it is not as simple as was once thought. Several genes come into play, making almost any combination of parent-and-child eye color possible.

Ears
Inheritance affects size and shape, the likelihood of some hearing impairments or diseases, free or attached earlobes, and even whether earwax is wet or dry.

What are traits?
Genetic traits are inherited characteristics passed from parents to children. Genes affect traits all over our body, for example, how tall we are, whether we have straight or curved thumbs, and even whether or not we can roll our tongue.

Smile
Inheritance affects many features of your smile, from the fullness of your lips to the size of your teeth, to whether or not you have dimples.

Chin
Genes control many chin features, including how much beard you grow. A simple gene inheritance also controls whether you have a cleft or partially divided chin.

Similarities in siblings
Brothers and sisters share physical traits because they have the same parents. Even if they have only one parent in common, siblings can share a variety of traits passed on from that common parent. Identical twins have almost exactly the same genes, which is what makes them look so similar.

Genetic Facts

nherited traits are passed on through genes. There is a full set of a person's genes in every cell of their body, with the exception of the reproductive cells (eggs and sperm), which have only half a set, and in red blood cells, which do not have genes at all.

We get our genes from our parents—half from our mother and half from our father. In turn, if we have children, we pass half of our genes to each of them, combining them with whoever is the other parent. This mixing of genes is part of what keeps human populations and other living creatures robust.

Nucleus

Ribosomes

Mitochondrion

Chromosom

Endoplasmic
reticulum

Golgi
apparatus

Instructions for how to behave
Genes are instructions for how individual cells should be built and then behave. This is how muscle cells and brain cells, which have the same genes, know to be constructed and behave differently.

Where genes are found
Located in the center of a cell is the cell nucleus. The nucleus contains the cell's chromosomes, which in turn contain thousands of genes. Because it contains the genetic material, the nucleus is sometimes thought of as the cell's control center.

Dominant and recessive
What happens if each parent gives a child different genes for the same trait, for example, cleft chin and no cleft chin? It turns out that certain gene traits are stronger, or dominant, and weaker, or recessive. The dominant gene is the one that is expressed.

Brown eyes are usually dominant gene traits.

Blue eyes are usually recessive gene traits.

Inheritance vs. environment

While some traits are determined by genes, it is also true that some traits from genes are affected by the environment. Skin color, for example, is controlled initially by genes. But if you go out in the sun, this exposure to the environment will redden or darken your skin color. Factors such as diet, exercise, and living situation can all affect how genes express themselves.

Nose shape is not easily affected by environment, but skin color is.

DNA

Chromosome

DNA structure

Genes are made of a substance called deoxyribonucleic acid, or DNA. This long, ribbon-like molecule is made up of various chemicals that form a chain similar to rungs of a spiraling ladder.

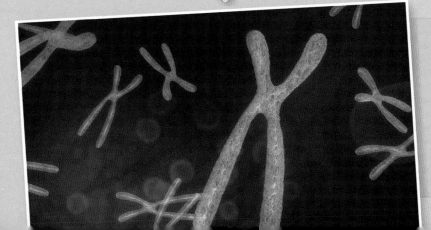

Chromosomes pairs

Humans have 23 pairs of chromosomes in every cell, giving 46 chromosomes in all. Half of each pair comes from the mother and half from the father. The 25,000 or so genes on these chromosomes make us who we are.

Genes and Inheritance

The traits inherited by a child depend both on genetics and a bit of chance. The reproductive cells, or sperm and egg, of both the man and woman have half the usual number of chromosomes in a cell. There is no particular rule for which genes end up in any given reproductive cell. It is also chance as to which two reproductive cells will actually join.

When these reproductive cells come together to form a zygote, the chromosomes from the mother and father splice together to form a unique individual with a unique combination of traits from both parents.

1 Reproductive cells
The reproductive cells of both men and women have only half the usual number of chromosomes. When the sperm and egg come together, they each contribute half of the 46 chromosomes that form the person.

Alleles

Everyone has two copies of each gene for each trait. Each copy is called an allele. When a reproductive cell is formed, only one allele for each trait goes into it.

2 Developing zygote
The zygote cell begins to reproduce itself by dividing in two. These cells, in turn, begin dividing to reproduce themselves. This is the start of the process of forming a new body.

3 Specializing cells
As development continues, genetic information instructs cells to begin specializing into different organs. This allows the body's more mature form to take shape.

The same for everyone
Each cell in the human body has 23 pairs of chromosomes, or 46 chromosomes altogether.

HEREDITY

Everyone has two copies of every gene. The top rows of this diagram show the father's genes (red and green) and the middle rows show the mother's (blue and orange). These genes combine in their baby (bottom rows) so half the genes come from each parent. If the same couple had another child, the father's and mother's rows would be the same, but the combination in the baby's rows would be different.

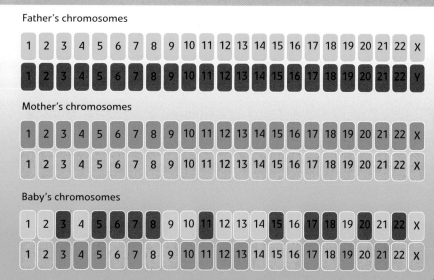

Father's chromosomes

| 1 | 2 | 3 | 4 | 5 | 6 | 7 | 8 | 9 | 10 | 11 | 12 | 13 | 14 | 15 | 16 | 17 | 18 | 19 | 20 | 21 | 22 | X |

| 1 | 2 | 3 | 4 | 5 | 6 | 7 | 8 | 9 | 10 | 11 | 12 | 13 | 14 | 15 | 16 | 17 | 18 | 19 | 20 | 21 | 22 | Y |

Mother's chromosomes

| 1 | 2 | 3 | 4 | 5 | 6 | 7 | 8 | 9 | 10 | 11 | 12 | 13 | 14 | 15 | 16 | 17 | 18 | 19 | 20 | 21 | 22 | X |

| 1 | 2 | 3 | 4 | 5 | 6 | 7 | 8 | 9 | 10 | 11 | 12 | 13 | 14 | 15 | 16 | 17 | 18 | 19 | 20 | 21 | 22 | X |

Baby's chromosomes

| 1 | 2 | 3 | 4 | 5 | 6 | 7 | 8 | 9 | 10 | 11 | 12 | 13 | 14 | 15 | 16 | 17 | 18 | 19 | 20 | 21 | 22 | X |

| 1 | 2 | 3 | 4 | 5 | 6 | 7 | 8 | 9 | 10 | 11 | 12 | 13 | 14 | 15 | 16 | 17 | 18 | 19 | 20 | 21 | 22 | X |

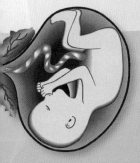

4 At birth
A fully developed baby has a unique set of genes received in part from the mother and in part from the father. The expression of that combination of genes is seen in the traits the child displays once it is born.

Chromosome numbers

Different living things have different numbers of chromosomes in their cells. Chromosome number alone does not identify a species, nor does it say much about the organism. The magic is in the genes carried on those chromosomes.

Species	Chromosomes
Pea plant	14
Sunflower	34
Cat	38
Puffer fish	42
Human	46
Dog	78
Carp	104

Diving into Genes and DNA

Genes tell each of the body's cells what to do and when to do it, for example, "be a liver," "make heart tissue," or "carry nerve signals." Genes do this by making particular proteins. Each gene is, in fact, a recipe for making a certain protein at a certain time.

DNA is formed by a pair of tightly bonded molecules, and genes are sections or segments of those molecules. The DNA molecule's shape is a double helix, similar to a twisted ladder. The sides of the ladder are phosphate and sugar groups. The rungs of the ladder are called base pairs because they are always built from pairs of chemicals called nucleotides. These base pairs are made up of two of four nucleotides called adenine, thymine, guanine, and cytosine.

DNA alphabet

The base pairs of adenine (A), thymine (T), guanine (G), and cytosine (C) form the genetic alphabet. Genetic traits are created by the combinations of letters of this alphabet, that is, the way the base pair groups are formed. For example, a string of base pairs with the sequence ATCGTT might be the combination for blue eyes, while a similar but different string in the same position on the DNA strand, such as ATCGCT, might give brown eyes.

Base pairs
The base pair rungs of the DNA double helix are the alphabet of genetics. Combinations of these base pairs give us our traits.

That's Amazing!
Across the 46 chromosomes that humans have in their cells, there are approximately 3 billion base pairs making up our genes.

Twisting double helix
The DNA helix usually twists to the right. If you took a single molecule of DNA and stretched it to its full length, it would be more than 3 feet (1 m) long.

Bases in a gene
The average gene is formed by around 3,000 bases. Some are shorter, others longer. The largest human gene is made up of 2.4 million bases.

BASE PAIRING

The rungs of the DNA ladder are formed following two simple rules: adenine (A) always pairs with thymine (T), and cytosine (C) always pairs with guanine (G). Sometimes one will be on the left side of the ladder and sometimes on the right, but they always combine in these specific pairs, joined by a hydrogen bond.

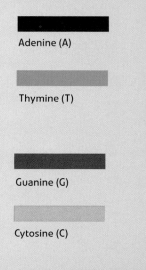

Adenine (A)

Thymine (T)

Guanine (G)

Cytosine (C)

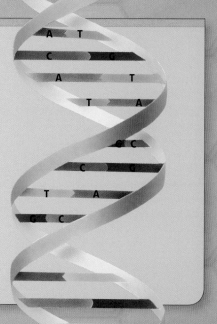

A   T
C   G
A   T
T   A
G C
C   G
T   A
G C

DNA Replication

All the time, in every part of the body, cells are dividing to create new cells. However, both cells have to have a full set of DNA chromosomes to be correctly formed. Most cells deal with this by splitting the DNA in half and creating a full duplicate of the DNA molecules.

Because of base pairing, each half of the split DNA molecule has all the information it needs to create a new copy. If the split rung is an A, then it attracts a spare T floating around in the cell nucleus, and vice versa. If the unpaired base is a C, then it attracts a spare G, and vice versa.

Mitosis and meiosis

There are two kinds of cell division. In mitosis, a parent cell splits, creating two daughter cells that are identical to the parent. These cells are used by the body to grow and repair itself. In meiosis, the daughter cells have half the number of chromosomes of the parent cell. The result of meiosis is reproductive cells.

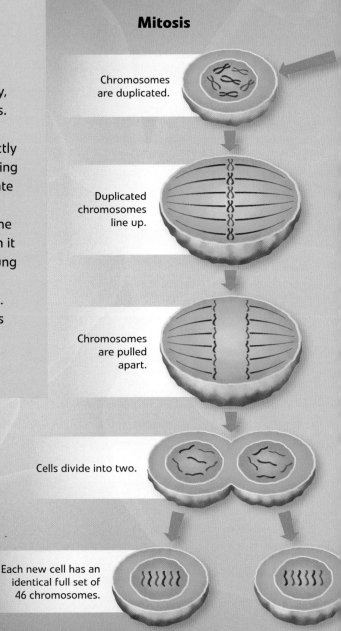

Mitosis

Chromosomes are duplicated.

Duplicated chromosomes line up.

Chromosomes are pulled apart.

Cells divide into two.

Each new cell has an identical full set of 46 chromosomes.

Meiosis

Parent cell

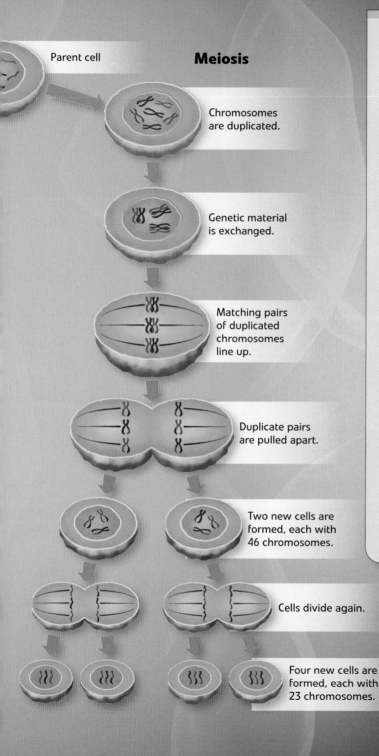

Chromosomes are duplicated.

Genetic material is exchanged.

Matching pairs of duplicated chromosomes line up.

Duplicate pairs are pulled apart.

Two new cells are formed, each with 46 chromosomes.

Cells divide again.

Four new cells are formed, each with 23 chromosomes.

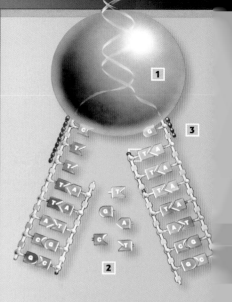

SPLITTING DNA

1 Enzymes break the chemical bond between the base pairs, similar to a zipper unzipping.

2 Spare nucleotides in the cell nucleus bond to the now-unpaired bases. If the unzipped nucleotide is a G, a C bonds to it. If the unzipped nucleotide is a C, then a G bonds to it. It is the same process for A and T.

3 Extra phosphates and sugars join the base pairs together, forming the rest of the DNA ladder.

Did You Know?

Cells divide faster when you are a child because you are growing. When you are an adult, cell division slows down and is focused mainly on repair and maintenance work.

DNA Facts

Sugar and phosphate

The sides of the DNA ladder are made up of sugar and phosphate molecules. Bases attach to the sugar molecules, and a complete nucleotide has a base, a sugar, and a phosphate.

DNA variations

If you look at the genes of any two humans, you will find that they are 99.9 percent the same. This means that all genetic differences between each human come from just 0.1 percent of our genes.

Same but different

Double helix

DNA's twisted ladder, or double-helix, shape was first understood by two biochemists named James Watson and Francis Crick. They figured it out by looking at an X-ray photo of a DNA sample. Their research won them a Nobel Prize.

James Watson

Francis Crick

Red blood cells

Mature red blood cells are the only cells in the body that do not contain any DNA. This is because a mature red blood cell does not have a nucleus, so there is no associated DNA.

That's Amazing!

DNA is a very tiny 2 nanometers across, which is between 25,000 and 50,000 times thinner than a single strand of human hair.

Journey to the Sun and back

If you took all your DNA and laid it out end to end, it would stretch to the Sun and back about 300 times.

External factors

Environmental and behavioral influences can turn genes on and off. For example, what you eat can affect how your genes create or fight a disease such as cancer. An unhealthy diet inhibits cancer-fighting genes, while a healthy diet can trigger genes to fight the disease.

Healthy diet

Unhealthy diet

Milestones

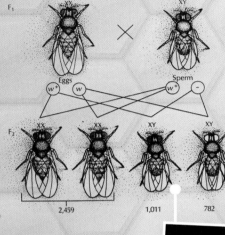

Our understanding of genetics did not happen overnight. It was built over decades, one discovery at a time and one insight at a time. Researchers have spent lifetimes working on the problems of genetics.

It was not until the 1800s that scientists began to understand how genetic inheritance works. Significant milestones include proposing natural selection, working out that genes are found on chromosomes, and how the genetic code works.

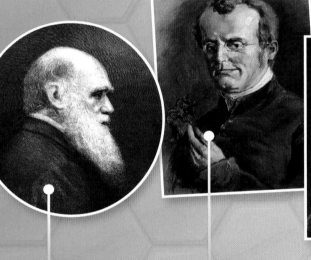

1858
The theory of natural selection—that species that adapt to their environment survive to pass on their inherited traits—was described by British naturalist Charles Darwin.

1866
Austrian priest and botanist Gregor Mendel published the results of his inheritance experiments on pea plants. This showed that the passing on of traits follows specific natural laws.

1905
William Bateson, a British scientist, coined the term "genetics." He discovered Mendel's work in 1900 and found it explained his own research findings in plant inheritance.

1910
American zoologist Thomas Hunt Morgan's experiments with fruit flies showed that genes on chromosomes are responsible for passing on hereditary traits.

941

mericans George Beadle
nd Edward Tatum (first
nd second from left)
howed that genes affect
eredity by acting on
nzymes. Their joint work
on a Nobel Prize in 1958.

1953

James D. Watson, an
American biochemist
and geneticist, and British
biochemist Francis Crick
figured out that DNA
has the structure of a
double helix.

1977

The world's first genetic
engineering company,
Genentech, was founded.
It made new drugs using
genetic engineering—
splicing together genes
from different organisms.

1989

British geneticist Alec
Jeffreys first used the term
"DNA fingerprinting" and
created methods that use
DNA to solve crimes and
determine paternity (who
a child's father is).

The Human Genome Project

Wide-ranging research
The areas of study involved in the Human Genome Project included chemistry, biology, physics, ethics, informatics, and engineering.

The Human Genome Project was a major international scientific research project designed to map the human genome. It aimed to look at each of the 23 chromosome pairs and identify the location and function of all 25,000 or so genes, as well as all 3 billion base pairs. The project also looked into technical, ethical, legal, and social issues raised by the research. It is still one of the biggest scientific investigations ever conducted.

Beginning in 1990, the multibillion dollar project was originally expected to find 100,000 genes and take 15 years. However, there turned out to be fewer genes than expected, and computer technology improved, allowing them to finish the mapping two years ahead of schedule, in 2003.

An international effort

The Human Genome Project was led by the US Department of Energy and the National Institutes of Health, but it soon became an international undertaking. Other participating countries included:

Australia	Germany	Netherlands
Brazil	Israel	Russia
Canada	Italy	Sweden
China	Japan	United Kingdom
Denmark	Korea	
France	Mexico	

Mapping a chromosome

One key result of the Human Genome Project is a far greater understanding of specific genes on specific chromosomes. Below is a representation of Chromosome 1 (of 23), which contains 246 million base pairs. The labels show approximately where some of the genes controlling specific diseases and traits reside on the chromosome. These are just some of the hundreds of genes that a full mapping would show.

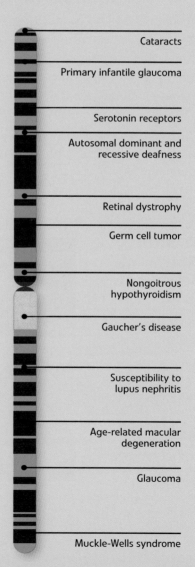

Cataracts

Primary infantile glaucoma

Serotonin receptors

Autosomal dominant and recessive deafness

Retinal dystrophy

Germ cell tumor

Nongoitrous hypothyroidism

Gaucher's disease

Susceptibility to lupus nephritis

Age-related macular degeneration

Glaucoma

Muckle-Wells syndrome

Mutations

The cells in our bodies are dividing all the time and usually make exact copies of themselves. But sometimes a cell does not succeed in getting the DNA copy 100 percent correct. Sometimes this is a naturally occurring error. At other times, the changes are caused by outside influences, such as radiation or viruses. Any changes to an organism's DNA sequence are called mutations.

There are many different kinds of mutations. In substitution mutations, a base pair letter is changed, for example, there is an A instead of a G. Insertion mutations see extra base pairs added in the DNA sequence. Deletion mutations are when a chunk of the DNA is lost.

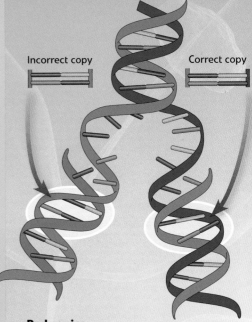

Incorrect copy   Correct copy

Bad copies
Mutations are the result of incorrect copying of DNA. This can happen anywhere along the DNA molecule, although there are "hot spots" that are 100 times more likely to be the site of a mutation.

GOOD, BAD, OR INDIFFERENT

The word "mutation" brings up images of deformed and sick beings. These do occur, but not all mutations are bad. Some are neutral and some are beneficial. A neutral mutation might change a color or texture of an organism, but not have any effect on its ability to survive. A beneficial mutation improves survivability. For example, if a mutated animal can hide from predators better because of a change in skin color, that trait will probably get passed on.

Extra horns
A genetic mutation caused this goat to have extra horns.

Different eye color
This cat's DNA has given it eyes with different colors.

Extra head
The extra head on this turtle is not a beneficial mutation.

Causes
Mutations can be caused by factors outside the body. These include exposure to particle radiation (as a result of a nuclear power plant accident), electromagnetic radiation (X-rays or UV rays from the Sun), and certain chemicals and viruses. These can cause cells to change how they replicate.

Cancer
Cancer occurs when cells develop abnormally and grow uncontrollably (seen here in blue). A cancerous cell results from a series of mutations to a single cell. It is very unlikely that any given cell will ever mutate. So it is even more unlikely that a single cell will mutate several times, as in the case of cancer, but it does happen. Cancer is more likely in older people because their cells have more time to undergo a series of mutations.

Did You Know?
Fast and frequent mutation can help an organism evolve and survive. This is seen, for example, in bacteria that become resistant to antibiotics.

How to Be a Geneticist

The field of genetics has boomed in the past few decades. As a result, the opportunities for people interested in science and working in a field covering heredity, mutation, cell growth, and reproduction have grown. Geneticists do more than simply look through a microscope. Genetics jobs range across medicine, agriculture, and science, and include work in medical genetics, genetic counseling, gene therapy, organ transplants, fertility, reproduction, genetic modification of food, animal breeding, biotechnology, drugs, forensics, teaching, gene testing, and law. In other words, there is plenty of scope in genetics for a wide range of interests.

Special interest
Different laboratories work on different kinds of genetics. Once you identify what area of genetics interests you, such as forensics or bioinformatics, and you get an appropriate education, you need to find a laboratory that works in your area of interest.

Studying genetics can lead to a career finding and curing genetic diseases.

Education

Geneticists must study at universities, usually for several years. They start by earning a bachelor's degree, usually in a science such as biology or chemistry. Later, they may study for a master's degree and a doctorate, or PhD.

Fieldwork and research

Most geneticists do research as part of their studies. For someone working in the genetics of agriculture, for example, there is no substitute for seeing genetics applied to living plants.

A WEEK IN THE LIFE OF A CLINICAL GENETICIST

Clinical geneticists are medical doctors who are also trained in genetics, often specializing in childhood diseases. They work to identify and investigate genetic disorders and what risks these might pose to a family. They might also counsel couples on the risk of passing on genetic disorders to any children they might have.

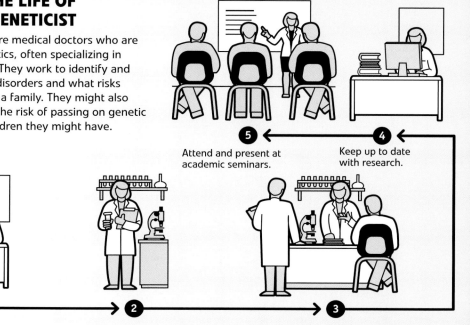

5 Attend and present at academic seminars.

4 Keep up to date with research.

1 Meet with clients in clinic.

2 Conduct research in a laboratory.

3 Lead laboratory meetings.

DNA Fingerprinting

Also called DNA profiling, DNA fingerprinting is used to identify someone or something, for example a particular animal species or an individual person. Since the DNA from any two human beings is 99.9 percent the same, DNA fingerprinting uses the 0.1 percent that is not the same to identify unique characteristics of the person profiled. It focuses on short pieces of the genetic code that repeat for a given person and distinguish them from everyone else.

This kind of genetic analysis can be a useful legal and forensic tool to help find out whether someone was involved in a crime or has responsibility in a situation, such as a paternity suit.

Solving crimes

DNA left behind at the scene of a crime can be used to identify who was present and involved. Hair, blood, saliva, and skin cells all contain samples of someone's DNA.

That's Amazing!

DNA fingerprinting was first used in 1986 in the UK to solve a murder case. DNA testing cleared the main suspect and helped find the real culprit.

Identifying dead bodies

DNA profiling can be used to identify people who have died but whose identity is not known, such as soldiers killed in action, people killed in natural disasters, or a corpse found at the scene of a crime.

Protecting endangered species

A genetic analysis of plants and animals gives different information about the species compared to studying their outward appearance. This genetic information can be used to identify members of an endangered species that need protecting.

Macaws are endangered birds.

Diagnosis of disorders

DNA profiling allows doctors to diagnose inherited diseases such as hemophilia, cystic fibrosis, Huntington's disease, familial Alzheimer's, and sickle cell anemia. Early detection can lead to successful treatment or management.

Clubbing fingertips can be a sign of cystic fibrosis, but DNA profiling can detect this disease much sooner.

Confirming paternity

Where there is a question of who has fathered a child, a genetic test that compares the father's DNA to the child's can determine paternity. This has legal implications for who is responsible for supporting the child.

?... You Decide

Genetic engineering takes genes from one living organism and puts them into another to change it and achieve some purpose. This might be to improve the disease resistance of crops or increase the shelf life of food. The effects of genetic engineering are hotly disputed. Most genetic practices have both pros and cons.

Age-old practice
Farmers have been manipulating crop and livestock genes for centuries, via selective breeding, to improve results. Science can now take this a step further by manipulating the genes directly.

Fact or Fiction?
Can genetic engineering make your children smarter, more athletic, and better looking? Some think genetic engineering of this kind would kill us, but the answer is not yet known.

Treating disease
The ability to treat certain diseases may be improved by creating genetically modified drugs and drug delivery systems within the body. Gene therapy, where a person's genes are changed to treat disease, could be a blessing for people who suffer certain diseases.

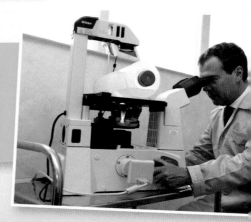

Easing world hunger
By genetically engineering crops, more food could be produced more reliably, which can help feed more people around the planet. Also, crops could be created to better meet the needs of farming in certain areas.

Contaminating crops

Once genetically modified crops are used, they can contaminate the crops of nearby farmers who do not want to use them. Their spread can be uncontrolled, and no one knows for sure what their effects on nature will be.

Seed monopoly

Companies that create genetically modified crops can patent their seeds, meaning farmers would have to buy seeds only from them. This monopoly takes away the farmers' freedom to buy seeds from whomever they want or to save their own seeds.

Threatened food supply

As more genetically engineered food makes it to the dining table, the long-term effects of eating them are still unknown. Some fear unexpected health consequences that might appear only when it is too late to go back.

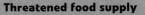

Glossary

allele (uh-LEEL) One particular version of a gene on a chromosome representing a specific trait or part of a trait. Alleles normally come in pairs: one inherited from the mother and one from the father.

base pair (BAYS PAYR) A pair of nucleotides that make up one rung of the DNA ladder.

biochemist (by-oh-KEH-mist) A scientist who studies the chemical compounds and processes in organisms.

chromosome (KROH-muh-sohm) A strand of DNA in a cell nucleus that carries an organism's genes. Humans have 46 chromosomes in their cells.

DNA (dee-en-AY) Short for deoxyribonucleic acid, this acid is found in the nucleus of cells that contains the body's genetic instructions.

DNA fingerprinting (dee-en-AY FING-ger-print-ing) The process of using DNA to identify someone or something.

dominant trait (DAH-mih-nent TRAYT) A genetic trait that tends to be stronger and more likely to be expressed in a person.

double helix (DUH-bul HEE-liks) The paired helix shape taken by DNA molecules.

enzymes (EN-zymz) Complex proteins produced by living cells that speed up chemical reactions.

gene (JEEN) The basic unit of heredity in a living organism.

genetic engineering (jih-NEH-tik en-juh-NIR-ing) The process of slicing up genes and splicing together parts of genes from different organisms.

geneticist (jih-NEH-tuh-sist) A person who studies or works with genes and genetics.

genetics (jih-NEH-tiks) The study of heredity in living organisms.

genome (JEE-nohm) The complete DNA sequence for a living organism.

helix (HEE-liks) A curve that winds around in a spiral, as if on the surface of a cylinder.

heredity (her-ED-uh-tee) The passing of traits from parents to offspring.

Human Genome Project (HYOO-mun JEE-nohm PRAH-jekt) An international research effort that mapped the genes found in humans.

inheritance (in-HEHR-uh-tens) The group of attributes a person has that biologically come from one's parents.

meiosis (my-OH-sis) A form of cell division where the parent splits into four daughter cells, each with 23 chromosomes instead of 46.

mitosis (my-TOH-sis) A form of cell division where a parent cell splits to form two daughter cells that are identical to the parent cell.

mutation (myoo-TAY-shun) A change to an organism's genetic structure.

nucleotide (NOO-klee-uh-tyd) One of the components that make up the rungs of the DNA ladder structure.

nucleus (NOO-klee-us) The center compartment of a cell that contains DNA and RNA (ribonucleic acid).

paternity (puh-TER-nih-tee)
The legal acknowledgment
that someone is the father
of a child.

protein (PROH-teen) Chemical
substances produced by DNA.

recessive trait
(rih-SEH-siv TRAYT) A genetic trait
that tends to be weaker and less
likely to be expressed in a person.

trait (TRAYT) A feature of a
living thing, like hair color or
fruit size.

zygote (ZY-goht)
The cell formed when a sperm
cell fertilizes an egg cell during
sexual reproduction.

Index

A

adenine 12–15

B

base pairs 12–13, 15, 20, 22
Bateson, William 18
Beadle, George 19

C

cancer 17, 23
cell division 14–15
cells 8, 10, 12, 14, 17, 22–23
chimpanzee genes 6
chin 7, 8
chromosomes 9, 10, 11, 14, 15,
    20, 21
Crick, Francis 16, 19
cytosine 12–15

D

Darwin, Charles 18
DNA 9, 12–13
    alphabet 12, 13
    fingerprinting 19, 26–27
    replication 14–15, 22
dominant genes 8
double helix 12, 13, 16, 19

E

ears 7
eggs 8, 10
endangered species 27
eyes 7, 22

G

Genentech 19
genetic engineering 19, 28–29
genetic inheritance 6–7, 18
genetic traits 6–8, 12, 18
geneticists 24–25
guanine 12–15

H

heredity 11, 19, 24
Human Genome Project 20–21

I

identical twins 7

J

Jeffreys, Alec 19

M

meiosis 14–15
Mendel, Gregor 18
mitosis 14
mutations 22–24

N

nucleotide 12, 15–16
nucleus 8, 14–15, 17

P

paternity 19, 21, 27
phosphate 12, 15–16

R

radiation 22–23
recessive genes 8
red blood cells 8, 17

S

smile 7
sperm 8, 10
sugar 12, 15, 16

T

thymine 12, 13, 14, 15
traits 6–10, 18, 21–22
twins 7

W

Watson, James D. 16, 19

Z

zygote 10

Websites

Due to the changing nature of Internet links, PowerKids Press has developed an online list of websites related to the subject of this book. This site is updated regularly. Please use this link to access the list: www.powerkidslinks.com/disc/dna/